# The Last of the
# ARCTIC

# The Last of the
# ARCTIC
## by William Kurelek

Pagurian Press Limited

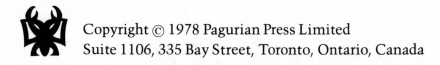
ISBN 0-88932-074-8

Printed and bound in Canada

To the white men,
missionaries,
traders,
government officials,
and others
who courageously faced
cold and privation
to give of themselves
beyond the call of duty
out of love
for the Inuit

# Contents

# Foreword

I was about halfway through the execution of the series of paintings reproduced in this book when it suddenly dawned on me: these too belonged with the series I'd been doing on the various ethnic groups that make up Canada. I have already done the Ukrainians and the Jews. The Irish and French Canadians will be done next year, then the Poles and Germans will have their settlement in Canada told in paint in 1977. Why hadn't I thought of the Eskimo in that light? In fact I'd probably not have done them at all had not Christopher Ondaatje, the publisher, approached me. He asked me to record the story of the Eskimos in thirty paintings before their identity was completely swamped by our southern white civilization. I guess the answer is that I simply hadn't thought of the Eskimo as an immigrant. He hadn't come from Europe as the others had to make this his country. He just seemed to belong here, as much a part of Northern Canada as snowdrifts, boulders, snowy owls, and seals. True, there's a theory that both the Eskimos and Indians had been immigrants when they'd come out of Asia across the Aleutian chain land-bridge, but that was many thousands of years ago and the facts are lost in pre-history. Today the Eskimos number only about 13,000 in Canada (though there are many more in Alaska and Greenland), because the barren North, vast as it is, cannot support a larger population.

Christopher Ondaatje has never been to the North himself, so I found his concern for the Eskimo rather strange. Although he comes from Ceylon it seems to me that he has imbibed a rather common romanticized notion of southern whites about the Eskimo. Perhaps we white men find it rather hard to love the Indian after fighting with him for this land, and, by default, the Eskimo has become our darling, so much so that we feel ourselves caught up in a kind of ecological crusade. We want to roll back the technological tide that threatens to obliterate the pristine Stone Age culture of the Inuit people. I can't recall the exact words of Chris' commission to me but, as if to affirm the thrust of his concern, he listed a dozen possible subjects for the book with the precautionary added request to "please avoid including skidoos, street lamps, car driving, telephone wires. I really want the Arctic captured as it was, before it is totally ruined by North American civilization."

I found myself in somewhat of a dilemma: I was quite willing to tackle the commission simply as a painting commission, but since Chris also expected stories to go with the pictures in his book, I had to admit to him that I didn't exactly share either his concern for, or his concept of, the Arctic. I had been to the Arctic some years earlier to do a series of landscapes around Cape Dorset on Baffin Island. There is an Eskimo Co-operative Art Centre at Cape Dorset that produces what are generally regarded to be the highest quality Eskimo soapstone carvings, prints, and weavings.

I saw at that time that most of the old Eskimo ways I'd read about had gone. Skidoos were everywhere, the equivalent of the family car of our own life style, and have replaced the dog sled in hunting. There were telephone and powerline poles on most of the main streets; big oil storage tanks provided heating fuel for

10

the whole community. Not a single igloo could be seen. The people now lived in prefabricated houses rented to them by the Canadian government at whatever price they could afford.

During that trip I stayed with Terry Ryan, then director of the Eskimo Art Co-op and Justice of the Peace, in his modern A-frame house equipped with every possible modern convenience. Had I not peered out of the window now and then to get the authentic color of the land for the paintings I was working on, I'd have felt I was back in a prosperous southern city. At mealtimes, only canned milk reminded me where I was.

On this trip I noticed that even more had changed. I write this in Pangnirtung which is on Baffin Island, a few miles south of the Arctic Circle. Every major Eskimo settlement now has an airstrip of its own with regular flight service interrupted only by bad weather. Satellite has brought color TV and FM radio and telephones right into the Eskimos' living rooms. I shopped several times at the Hudson's Bay store here. Apart from being much more compact, it resembles a chain store in the South rather than a fur trading post. At Peyton Lodge, where I am staying, only having to use a camp style toilet with green garbage bag reminds me that this building is standing on permafrost. It is obviously hopeless trying to find an authentic Stone Age Eskimo settlement to use as a model in this series even if I did have the time to explore. The landscape is still here, and Pangnirtung is truly beautiful as I was told it would be. Lacking authentic models, I made up my mind to quiz every white man and English-speaking Eskimo out here for information about the old ways of Arctic life. I have found books to be by far the greatest help: Kaj Birket-Smith's *Eskimos*, Bruemmer's *The Arctic*, and Duncan Pryde's *Nunaga* in particular.

So much for the difficulty in reconciling Chris' and my concepts of the actual appearance of the Arctic today. The philosophical discrepancy presents a much knottier problem. As I study these books I find myself in more general agreement with Birket-Smith and Pryde than with Bruemmer and Farley Mowat, another noted writer on the Arctic. But I can almost hear Bruemmer and Mowat saying as they look at this book, "The nerve of this fellow. Making pronouncements on the Arctic with only one month's actual experience of it." In a sense they would be right: I shouldn't be saying anything in this book, just doing illustrations for it. But in the broader human sense I disagree. Eskimos are human beings, not merely a higher species of Arctic animal. Therefore if I may legitimately produce a film deploring the plight of Third World peoples compared to our North American affluence, as I have, then I may just as legitimately express my opinion on the cultural and moral crises of the Eskimos. I therefore ask my readers to please remember that my disagreement with the nostalgic view of the Arctic has primarily to do with a broad view of mankind's destiny as a whole.

It is because I personally tend to look at any people in "world" terms that I feel like cheering when I read Farley Mowat's optimistic view of the Barrens as a source of protein foods, from caribou herds, for the burgeoning hungry populations of the world. In addition, tending of these herds would provide the Eskimo with employment which he so sadly lacks now. On the other hand I don't agree with Birket-Smith when he says that the most humane thing the Canadian Government can do for the Eskimo, now that we southerners have ruined his way of life, is to bring him South and assimilate him. I also don't agree with everything Pryde says in his books — one example being his views on personal morality—but on the whole, I have a good deal of respect for his common sense attitude to northern problems. He points out, for example, that the Eskimo is very pragmatic. He will not settle for a snow house after having lived

12

in a prefab. The Eskimo is quick to point out to the white man who suggests a return to the old ways, that *he* try living in a snow house. It is impossible to set the clock back. We cannot, to use another telling example, send all white men back to Europe so that the North American Indian can go back to *his* harmony with Nature. I myself caught a glimpse of a similar very serious problem in South Africa. The white man's subjugation of the Bantu is wrong, granted. But at the same time it would be irresponsible, in the total world context, to imagine that the natives can go back to zebra- and lion-hunting in the streets of Johannesburg.

It is only in his view of Arctic man's destiny in more worldly terms that I'm at odds with Bruemmer. I have nothing but admiration for his poetic sensitivity to the North, and his love for Arctic animals is particularly touching. I sympathize with his distress at the unnecessary suffering to Arctic wildlife that mere human vanity brings. But his talk of Nature as if it were God really distresses me, perhaps because it reminds me of the time when I used to confuse the two.

When you really get down to it, what is this "Nature" which people who hold this view are worshipping? Really, Nature of itself is nothing but a blind set of chemical and physical laws. It is not a person. It cannot plan or design anything. But it *is* a person, an infinitely wise and powerful Designer and Provider who created Nature. It was He who set Nature going and holds its every molecule in existence at every moment so that it works so efficiently. Bruemmer makes much of man being happiest and best equipped to survive when he is in harmony with Nature. With that I do agree. But I feel that to understand why the Eskimos are losing that harmony one must go deeper than Bruemmer's beautiful book. It is necessary to examine the total nature of man and evil. There is profound significance in the fact that it is man and man alone—he who is created in the image of God and has free will — who can and does sabotage the beautiful design God put into Nature. If there is no wider rationale to man's three-score-years-and-ten struggle to survive in the Arctic, then why worry? After all, Bruemmer himself in effect states that the Eskimos' thousands of years of magnificent struggle with the elements will be erased by the next Ice Age.

That brings me to Bruemmer's attitude to missionary work in the North. He states that missionaries replaced the culture of northern people who saw man essentially as an integral part of Nature with a new one that proclaimed man as Nature's master. Inevitably, he maintains, the cultural conflict produced an emotional dichotomy that continues to this day. Once again, it is all very well to aim at harmony with Nature. The church actually does back up this aim, if I understand correctly the recent Canadian Bishops' Labor Day message on northern development. They list five conditions to ensure both justice and respect for the Eskimo and Indian ways of life. Before any northern development project is allowed to proceed either by private enterprise or government, there must be (a) sufficient public discussion of it, (b) just land settlement with the natives, (c) effective participation of the natives in the development, (d) adequate measures to protect the terrain, and (e) control of energy resources to ensure plenty for the natives' own needs. God gave both Eskimos and white men intelligence. The one very intelligent decision that northern man has made, and white man should follow, is to work *with* nature, not *against* it — in other words to roll with its punches in development projects. But no Eskimo really wants to go back to a mere animal kind of harmony with Nature (as Duncan Pryde astutely observes).

The real tragedy, as I see it, occurs when the Eskimo is affected by white man's secular culture without the saving

14

grace of the missionaries' message. That message is the only one that makes sense to man's struggle to survive both on a physical and moral plane. It promises a happy and glorious end to all men equally, whether North or South. That is why, to me, the hope of the Eskimo lies not in Bruemmer's romanticism but in the ordination of the four young Eskimo priests I saw on TV here in Pangnirtung. And I believe that our white man's guilt feelings are wasted if we are to channel all our energy into ecological work while turning a blind eye to the bad example of our increasingly corrupt southern society. These are the deepest wounds we inflict on the Inuit people—every suggestive movie we send up there, every magazine glorifying our overindulgence in food and drink, every government official or company man obviously up North to make a quick buck. I have seen an Eskimo audience at a community hall movie cheer when Hollywood cowboy heroes gun down yet another Indian. And I have heard Eskimo children, lounging in the hotel and shopping center complex at Frobisher Bay, shout the filthiest of adult white man's language. In both the long and short run, we do more harm to our Eskimo brothers if the TV programs we beam in to them via satellite condone shoddy morality than if our starchy foods rot their teeth.

I realize of course that my views are perhaps not the standard sentiments one expects to find in a book about the Arctic. But if I'm to say anything at all—and I did offer to say nothing—then I feel it should be honest. I must say I admire Chris' tolerance of my views. And then, of course, each reader is free to decide for him or herself which view, if any, to accept.

*October, 1975*
*Pangnirtung*
*Northwest Territories*

# The Last of the
# ARCTIC

# Anxious Wife Peering into Blizzard

I was pleased to discover in my research that I had already experienced something of Arctic winters by virtue of having been raised on a farm in the Canadian prairies. Many's the time I had to flail my arms to bring back circulation to numbed fingers, and to wiggle my toes furiously to revive them after standing still for a long while in the snow. Out west, adults were known to freeze to death in their cars when stranded between farmhouses, and children sometimes lost their way to or from school in a blizzard, even with all the modern amenities. Until recently, however, the Eskimo had no one to rely on except himself when facing such merciless winters. Only gradually has the white man taken it on himself to rescue northern natives whenever they fell into serious trouble. In 1962, when an epidemic killed all the sleigh dogs on Baffin Island, the government brought all the Eskimos of the Island into Pangnirtung to live out the winter, while the dog population was re-stocked from other parts of the Arctic. Even as recently as seventy-five years ago, the Eskimo would simply have starved in such a situation. The North is so vast and the Eskimo population so sparse that the people could not dominate Nature as white man did, and had to live as harmoniously as they could with the forces of Nature. They didn't bother to try fighting the snow; they lived with it, took risks with it. A hunter going out in winter knew he might never return. He had no weather forecasts, no radio, no morning paper. He tried reading the sky as best he could, and then set out. Many a wife waited in vain for her man to return.

# The Stone Church at Pelly Bay

I was captivated by this simple, beautiful structure when I came across a black and white photograph of it in a government magazine, because it blended so well with the land. The church was built by Father Henry, a Catholic missionary. Father Henry and his companion, Father Goussart, according to Arctic writer Duncan Pryde, were splendid examples of the type of Arctic missionaries anyone could admire, always visiting the sick and in general working tirelessly for the good of the people.

The Canadian Arctic is divided roughly in two in terms of mission: the Anglicans in the east and the Catholics in the west. I myself visited Canon Mike Gardener's Anglican Native Training Center here in Pangnirtung. At his home the next day I watched the ordination of four of his pupils on television, the ceremony conducted in the Eskimo language. It was the Anglican missionaries who gave the Eskimos a written language, incidentally. I liked the nice homely atmosphere of the ordination, where I could see Eskimo women carrying babies on their backs into the Cathedral as I'd seen it done around the smaller settlements. The Cathedral in Frobisher Bay is built in the shape of an igloo. As I was pulling on my overshoes in the porch after the show, an Eskimo, obviously a carpenter, made a point of coming up to me and shaking my hand. He was the only Eskimo during my five weeks in the Arctic who welcomed me that way, and it made me feel at one with him. As I see it, brotherhood was possible between our two races in this particular instance because we had a common bond in the Faith.

# Eskimo Carving

A series of paintings called "The Last of the Arctic" is indeed a strange place to offer a painting about Eskimo carving. For it was the white man who nudged the Eskimo into producing carvings and prints for the people of the South. This happened as recently as the 1950's. Before then, the Eskimos were too busy eking out their survival; the few carvings they did do were transportable miniatures. It was, in fact, James Houston, the father of John Houston who is staying with me here in the lodge at Pangnirtung, who brought some soapstone carvings South in 1947 and started the Eskimo art craze. Printmaking was totally foreign to the paperless culture of the Eskimo. James Houston introduced that to the Arctic too, after a visit to Japan in the nineteen-fifties.

I have seen Eskimos working in soapstone in Cape Dorset and here in Pangnirtung. They prefer to work outside. The fellow I saw here had built himself a makeshift awning of packing cardboard. I know it was makeshift for the next day it was blowing snow and his whole studio was a shambles; I barely recognized the block of wood he'd been using for a seat.

An Eskimo boy came to my door here at the lodge and tried to sell me a bird, which he said his mother had carved. I jumped at the chance to meet this woman and offered to come to his home the next day to buy several pieces and see her working. He didn't turn up, but the episode served to remind me that some of the best Eskimo prints are produced by women.

An Eskimo starts work by examining a piece of soapstone to see what animal, bird, or human shape is suggested. He then roughs out the main shape with a hatchet, executing the detail with rasps and files which are often homemade. The filings from the soapstone itself are used as polishing grit.

# Hunter Awaiting Seal at Breathing Hole

This is a description of one kind of Eskimo seal hunt. After the ice had become thick enough on the sea to support his weight, the Central Eskimo in the old days set out with his dog team to find the breathing holes. A seal is a mammal and must surface for air every ten minutes or so. This is when its chief enemies, man and the polar bear, can catch it if they are stealthy enough. To be able to keep a series of breathing holes, the seal must continually resurface in each to prevent the ice forming a thick crust over the opening. Such breathing holes are called "agloos" and resemble tiny molehills. There is an inch-wide hole at the top usually covered with rime, the frozen breath of the seal.

After the dogs discover an agloo, the hunter scrapes away the rime with his knife to examine the larger hole below and determine from which angle the seal will approach. Then he carefully reconstructs the agloo and includes in it an ingenious indicator, a piece of bird's down tied to a thread, which hangs down into the hole. The slightest movement of the down tells the hunter a seal has arrived. The wait may take hours, or even days, because the seal has several breathing holes. Patience is the supreme virtue here, and even if the temperature goes down to fifty or sixty degrees below zero, he must sit perfectly still, for the mere squeak of packed snow underfoot might frighten away the seal.

In the central Arctic, the hunter sits on a block of snow. When the down trembles, indicating the presence of a seal, the hunter thrusts a harpoon downward with all his might. The harpoon is made so that the head detaches itself but is still attached to a cord which the hunter pulls on to land the seal. It is then dispatched with a club. There are many other ways in which the Eskimo catches seals, the various methods depending on the season and the animal's habits.

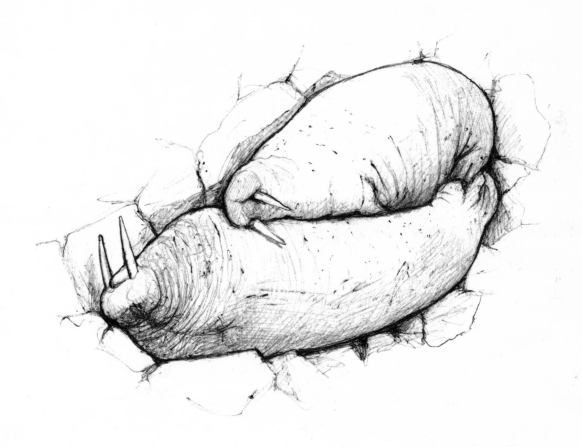

# The Urine Bowl

Although this picture may shock some readers, it ought not to. It's important to understand how the hygiene of the Eskimo was conditioned by his fierce struggle to survive. After a porch was built on a snow house, shelves were added on each side of it and anyone needing to urinate didn't have to go out into the bitter cold — one would use a special bowl set on one of the shelves for that purpose.

The Eskimo, as a rule, wasted nothing. Urine, for example, was used for washing because too much precious blubber would have been needed to melt enough snow for that purpose. Eskimo women in Greenland also used urine for bleaching their hair and curing skins. Greenlandic men going out to hunt would sometimes scent themselves with urine in the belief that animals, attracted by the smell of a maiden (suggested by the urine), would allow themselves to be caught.

The rest of the shelves held such items as meat dishes, blubber oil trays, tool trays and rolled-up skins. One might have even found a bitch, with puppies too young to stand the cold outside, in the space below. And of course women accommodated their personal items on such shelves, much as southern women do on their pantry and bedroom dressers, while men found them handy for storing hunting equipment.

# Arctic Madonna and Child

This painting may have the appearance of a pleasant Christmas card, but I mean it to be more: a philosophical and theological statement. Some thinkers and writers on the Arctic argue that the advent of white missionaries dislocated the life of the Eskimo. My contention is that it was only temporary dislocation. I also contend that this dislocation, whatever there was of it, would have occurred anyway from other political philosophies as white exploration pushed inevitably northward. The only question is which southern philosophy is the right one. My own commitment to the Christian faith has saved my life and given it meaning and purpose. I have depicted the Christ child in Mary's arms fondling one of His creations, a husky pup. As recorded in Genesis, God made every sort of wild beast and all the different kinds of cattle and creeping things; "and God saw it and found it good." The hunter is Joseph, pegging down the dog team for the night. For a setting, instead of the rough shelter of the stable at Bethlehem, we have the quick shelter of snow blocks, thrown up by Eskimo hunters. And instead of the star-spangled desert skies of the Middle East, we have the incredibly beautiful Arctic artistry of the Creator of the Universe, the Northern Lights. The display of Northern Lights or *Aurora borealis* is something I miss here at Pangnirtung.

The whites here tell me that the strongest band of Northern Lights' activity is in the western Arctic, from Hudson Bay across to Alaska. I myself once saw a whole sky full of these dancing, bewitching nuances of color in Northern Ontario. It was so breathtaking, the only truly appropriate reaction seemed to be to whisper an Alleluia.

# A Hunter's Snow Shelter

Today, about the only time one sees an igloo being built is when a hunter erects a low shelter for protection against the elements during the night. These can be erected in as little as forty-five minutes, which is just as well, because if a hunter's journey takes him away from his more modern home for more than a day or two he has to build several shelters before his return.

I ran into problems with this picture because of contradictory information I had been given. Placing the hunter inside the igloo was fine, but John Houston pointed out that I couldn't leave the sled outside, sitting on its runners. The reason? If the dogs, still tethered to the sled, had seen an Arctic hare or fox or even a polar bear, they would have taken off across the snow, sled and all. We finally solved the problem by inverting the sled. This need not be a contrived solution, because a common chore hunters had to perform during stops was repairing damaged runners. To give the runners a final glaze, an Eskimo would fill his mouth with water and let it out in a thin stream along the runners. When the water hit the runner it would freeze.

After I had disposed of the possible runaway problem, John, who knows the Arctic because he grew up in Cape Dorset, still felt uneasy about the picture. The dogs couldn't be left alone for long, he pointed out, or they'd have eaten the leather traces. I

had to beat that problem by imagining that the dogs had just completed a big feast of seal or musk-ox meat and weren't interested in chewing their traces. Nowadays the problem would not occur because the traces are made of synthetic material such as nylon rope, but since the theme of this book is "the Arctic as it was" I couldn't honestly give nylon rope to a Stone Age hunter.

# Kayaks Towing Home a Narwhal

This might be a typical whaling camp scene, of former days, toward the end of winter. When the ice in the bay started breaking up, the Inuit tended to gravitate to the water's edge. They knew several kinds of whale, the bowhead, the grey, the beluga, and the narwhal, strangest of all. It was hunted and prized for the long, twisted, ivory tusk carried by the male. In the camp children would be playing, the women sewing or scraping skins, the men carving harpoon heads and harpoon throwing boards. But this quiet humdrum scene is deceptive: everyone had part of his attention on the sea. No sooner did someone spot a whale than the men ran down to the water, slipped into their kayaks and were off, the women and children shouting encouragement until the boats were out of earshot.

Most often the quarry submerged before they even reached it, but sometimes someone managed a successful ambush from behind an iceberg. Then all joined in to help. It is, after all, an ancient Eskimo custom to share game if it is large. A whale kill would mean food for many days for many people. The hunters would tow it in with their boats in tandem, to a tumultuous welcome from their women and children.

Once such a scene was a common sight, but whalers have been coming into the Arctic from outside for some four hundred years now, and whales are becoming scarce. Here at Pangnirtung some whale hunting was carried on into the 1950's. A herd of whale would be frightened by gunshot sounds at the head of the fiord so that they'd flee inland. Then when the tide ran out

the whales were stranded on the shoals just below the settle-ment here. It was easy then for both Eskimos and white man to simply walk up to them and slaughter them. Because of such over-killing (by men of all races), the Eskimos now are often forced to eat cheaper, starchy food imported from the South, as they can't always afford the high price of southern meat. One sad result of this is that they suffer the worst tooth decay of any people in the world.

# The Satiated Starvation Sleep

This picture derives from a story I read a long time ago which stuck tenaciously in my mind. I can't recall the book or newspaper it was in but it bore out the fact, for me at least, that there is a tendency in man to hibernate in cold climates just as there is in his anatomical cousin, the bear, whose skeleton and appetite are similar to man's.

It is also common for people to get drowsy after a heavy meal. So picture, if you will, an Eskimo family having been near starvation for a long time. In this picture I've imagined them to be living in Alaska or Greenland, where people dwelt in square houses partly built of rock and turf and lined with skins. I've imagined them making a large kill of, say, a walrus, and then gorging themselves for two or three days. Raw meat is much harder to digest than when it has been cooked—could they not then fall into a prolonged sleep inside the coziness of their underground hut? All that's really needed now is for one of the women to rouse herself occasionally to refill the blubber lamp and thus keep the house comfortably snug.

# Musk-Oxen Defending Young Against Blizzard

A musk-ox is a fascinating, impressive animal. A bull can weigh up to nine hundred pounds; both male and female have a pair of horns which lie flat against the head before curling out. But the animal's most distinctive feature is its coat of long, dark, brown-flowing hair that reaches almost to the ground. This makes it look like a huge, animated mop.

Like the caribou, musk-oxen also migrate, but only over short distances. The caribou may wander as far as eight hundred miles during a season, but musk-oxen in that time wander only a few miles between hill and valley. In summer they will be in the valleys eating grass and dwarf willow, but in the winter, when winds sweep snow into the valleys, the crust often becomes so hard that their hooves hardly dent the surface; then they must move up to higher ground where vegetation is scant, but a little more accessible.

I have painted such a herd at a hilltop in one of their characteristic defense positions. The musk-oxen's chief form of defense is to arrange themselves in a circle. This creates a tank-like bulwark which marauding animals can scarcely penetrate. If the enemy is a blizzard, as I've shown here, it is not necessary to form a full circle. In this case, the adults form a wedge, heads butted into the wind. The calves huddle behind their parents in relative calm and warmth waiting for the storm to subside. Their parents exhibit phenomenal endurance, often standing absolutely still, in wedge formation, for two or three days.

40

# Snowbank Fun

When I was a school boy on the Canadian prairies, the first I learned of the Eskimo was from our Grade Four geography book. In it, a classroom of children pretended to visit other children in various interesting foreign lands. The first people visited were the Eskimos, presumably because, although they inhabited a part of our country, they were totally apart from us in life style. Two features of an Eskimo child's life which I envied most were that children were never punished and never had to do chores, but could play all day. I too loved playing on top of snowbanks and tunneling through them, but this fun was always partly spoiled by the knowledge that it would be short-lived. My parents were strict: I was punished or scolded for any mischief whatsoever, and there were many chores to be done, even in winter. Most of the prairie children's truly "free play" was during recess at school, and as everyone knows that too is cut mercilessly short by the school bell.

Finally came the day when I too stood on the land of the Eskimos. This was at Cape Dorset. Before me was a huge snowbank, aswarm with rollicking, frolicking children. At first I thought I was reviewing my own childhood, but slowly I began to notice differences. I was amused to see that they didn't bother

with sleds or even pieces of cardboard as we'd always thought necessary, but would simply slide down on their bottoms. Here in Pangnirtung I notice also that some children use a single runner type of sled with handles that resembles a cross. I don't know if this shape of sled pre-dated the white man's advent but I've assumed it does and have included it in this painting.

I should end the notes on this picture by pointing out that Eskimo children's completely carefree days are now also gone. All children living in the main settlements must attend school today, as do their southern counterparts.

# Flensing a Walrus

This is the skinning job that Eskimo society assigned to menfolk. Perhaps it is typical of most primitive societies to have such a natural selection of male and female roles. I recall, at home on the farm in Manitoba with my Ukrainian parents, the unwritten rule that mother killed and prepared chickens, geese, turkeys. But father butchered the cows and pigs, and mother and we children helped only in the details of the slaughter — I have illustrated that family effort several times. There is another resemblance between that Ukrainian family picture and this one. It is that Arctic people of necessity had to work together because a single Eskimo, no matter how skilled, could not cope with the skinning and quartering of a large animal in frigid weather before it froze solid. It would then be unavailable for human consumption and the hunter's dogs would be allowed at it instead. As can be seen in the painting several men set to work as soon as the walrus was landed on the beach.

Everyone knew from long experience what to do, just as my father knew his job from his peasant upbringing in the old country. An Arctic slaughter, however, has one other big difference from a southern one. The animals we slaughtered in Manitoba had two main components to their carcasses — the outer shell, consisting of skin and bone and muscle, and the innards, that is the inner organs. Arctic animals present a third component to the butcher, namely blubber. All Arctic animals, with the exception of man himself, have a thick layer of fat between the skin and the bone and muscle, to insulate them against the cold. The whiteness of the flesh laid bare by the flensing in this

picture is really fat. As already mentioned, everyone knew he must work fast while the carcass was still warm—on a cold day one could actually see this warmth coming off as steam. A young boy is shown to one side drinking the warm blood in the cup of his hands, a thing I find revolting. It was hard enough for me, sensitive as I was, to handle the insides of a pig or chicken and I marvelled at the way my father, with his sleeves rolled up, attacked those inner organs without any aversion whatsoever.

Another reason for operating on the carcass right there on the beach was that it was well nigh impossible for Eskimos, with their limited transport equipment, to move such a large carcass for any distance once it had lost the buoying help of sea water. But when the walrus had been cut up each person would carry off as much as he could shoulder or load on a sled. In no time at all the whole carcass was in the settlement, distributed among the families.

# Stalking Migrating Caribou

The Eskimo used to hunt caribou not only for meat but also for the skin and fur. It is the best, being both lightweight and warm. Jackets made from it have only one disadvantage: hairs keep falling off into one's food. But if an Eskimo had to choose between warmth plus agility during the hunt, and eating hairs, he'd rather eat hairs.

Caribou is rarely hunted in deep winter, because its meat is then too lean and its fur too thick. If it is taken in winter then it is usually trapped in snow pits into which it is lured with the smell of human urine. The caribou goes after the salt in the urine. The best caribou hunting is in the summer or fall. Then they are attacked in kayaks at river fords towards which they are sometimes frightened by "inukshuks"—piles of rocks that resemble human forms, set on hillsides. In land hunting, women and children help out. First poles and piles of rocks are set up in a wedge-shaped trap. The women and children sneak up behind the herd and suddenly jump up with wolf-howls and waving arms. The herd flees down the corridor of poles until the animals are hopelessly jammed together in the wedge of rock piles, not daring to turn back. There they are slaughtered by the waiting menfolk.

In the picture a herd is shown after the first snowfall, heading back to the tree-line where there is more shelter and easier access to ground food. Hunters follow stealthily, sizing it up from concealment and making plans to get as many as possible.

The valley is still too shallow for inukshuks to be effective. Bow and arrow was the chief caribou hunting weapon before the white man introduced the rifle. The best materials Eskimos could find for bows in the old days were driftwood and deer antler. These were ingeniously pieced together and reinforced with layers of animal gut. But the age-long fight to survive in the Arctic has also made the Eskimo somewhat of a pragmatist. He cast no nostalgic backward glances at his bow once he observed the obvious superiority of the rifle.

# Sky Tossing at Alaskan Whaling Celebrations

The greatest celebrations among the Inuit people were those following a successful whale hunt, perhaps because the whale is the largest animal by far and might feed a whole settlement for a long time. On Hudson Bay, for example, such a celebration wasn't too complicated. After a whale kill men and women sat in circles in a big, open space and gorged themselves with a hearty meal of barely-cooked whale meat. Then all further work came to a halt while they lay about for several days digesting it. In Alaska, on the other hand, where part of the celebrations involved the trampoline-like sky toss, the whole idea was to honor the animal they'd just killed. It also had mimic mask dances and distribution of gifts among the people that represented the animals' generosity to them. It was all a kind of magic-making to gain the good will of the whale's soul and ensure further abundance during the rest of the season. Obviously the Eskimos of the west had a stronger sense of order than those of the east: If you alter something then you must make suitable recompense even if it is only in the nature of a ceremonial gesture.

The drums to be seen in this picture are the one musical instrument common to all Eskimos. It is actually a tambourine with a handle at its side. The drummer holds the instrument by that handle, rocking the taut skin on its axis from side to side

and alternately beating each side of the frame with a heavy stick. This starts off slowly but gradually picks up tempo. It is a hollow, mysterious sound and its monotony can batter the nerves till they seem near breaking point. The drummer doesn't stop there, but goes on and on evermore furiously until even the drum itself seems ready to break.

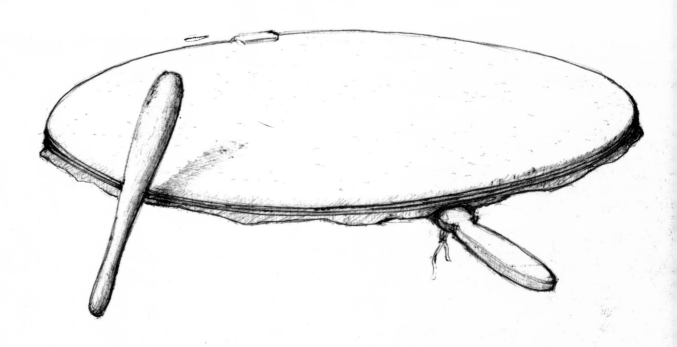

# Erqinanguartivarivna: How Awfully Sweet He Is!

In this painting we have a mother doting on her baby, surrounded by a group of admiring children. A caption for the picture might be this cuddling song from Greenland:

> *How awfully sweet he is*
> *Ayaya*
> *How awfully sweet he is and dear*
> *Ayaya*
> *That little wonder there!*

What I am trying to say with both the picture and song is that children in the Arctic are well cared for. A mother lavishes love and attention on her children, gives them the best selection of food and fabricates simple toys for them. She also prepares her children for their coming role in the family not so much by the use of force, that is by punishment or harsh verbal instructions, but by playing games with them, devised by herself, that reflect adult roles. The hood which carried the baby on the mother's back, in former days, was shaped so that the mother could quickly and easily shift her child from behind to the front for breast-feeding. Also, since the child lay easily along her back the mother could feel him begin the strain of elimination. In a twinkling the child found himself naked in the snow. (It's little wonder the Eskimos are such a hardy race.) Dried moss lined the bottom of the hood to absorb urine should there be an accident, and it was easily replaced.

Children up to the age of two are rarely disciplined, possibly because of the belief that through their names they are closely associated with dead relatives whom the mother misses. Discipline increases from the age of two until eight, from the time they can be naughty, until the time they can be ashamed of it. Community mores and code of ethics take over from that point.

# Igloo Building

Contrary to what most southerners believe the Inuit word *iglu* refers to any dwelling, not specifically to a snow house. In outlying regions of the Arctic where some wood is available for ceiling beams, "igloos" (a southern term) were also made of wood, turf, and skins, as well as snow. The simple snow house was developed out of several necessities and restrictions. In the Arctic, Nature is a harsh but effective teacher: The most abundant material of all is snow itself. White man finds it hard to believe but even Arctic animals know that it is actually a great insulator. There may be as much as a 60°F difference in temperature between the outside and inside of a snowbank.

In the old days before the advent of steel carpenters' saws, the Eskimo's chief house-building tools were simply a serrated antler and an ivory knife. He knows exactly what kind of wind-packed snow is suitable snowblock material. The blocks are sawed out rectangular in shape and laid on top of each other in an ascending spiral. The dug-out whence the blocks have been lifted serves as a sunken floor for the house. Invariably platforms are left on three sides of the circular floor plan, a wide one at the back serves as a common family bed and two smaller ones at the sides for cooking, sitting or working on. Each block is trimmed with the knife to fit snuggly to its neighbor and then pushed firmly into place with a blow of the fist. Each block is also sloped slightly inward so that the whole construction eventually comes to a domed peak. The last block of all, which contains a hole for ventilation, is cut in the shape of a jack-o-lantern top and serves as a keystone in Inuit architecture. Loose snow or chips of it are packed into the crevices.

This was the basic structure that could be raised in as little as an hour. It was already tolerably warm and comfortable, but many features could be and usually were added, depending on how long a community of Eskimos, essentially a nomadic people, stayed in one place. The first addition was a window, a slab of freshwater ice which replaced one of the blocks. A short low tunnel, which was entered on hands and knees, served as a wind-breaking tunnel. Another addition was a smaller side dome attached to the main one to serve as a storeroom and a kennel for the dogs. In fact in ambitious communities a whole complex of snowdomes with interconnecting tunnels would go up, somewhat like our modern indoor shopping plazas. Visiting between families could go on without outdoor exposure to wind and cold. Invariably all these dwellings lost their virginal interior whiteness from the smoke of many blubber lamps but there was never shortage of snow to build new igloos.

# Shaman at a Hudson Bay Holy Stone

This stone stands on Sentry Island on Hudson Bay's west coast. To it are tied cans of tobacco, baking powder, knives and the like, put there in relatively recent times to ensure good luck on a seal hunt. These are white man's objects of course; before white man came the Eskimo used amulets. These were so small though, they'd hardly have been seen in my picture so I doctored the timing a bit. Amulets varied greatly and expressed grotesque imagination and idea association. Thus owl claws gave the Eskimo strong fists during the hunt, caribou ears quick hearing, and lamp soot gave strength simply because soot outlived fire. A fish skin in the tool box assured good luck while fishing; the skin of a loon sewn into the side of a kayak gave it speed.

There were occasions, however, when it seemed such offerings were not sufficient and it was necessary to call in a shaman, who had special communication with supernatural forces. He was believed to carry within him a shining fire recognized by the spirits. He had the power to fight hostile spirits or, on the earthly level, to discover a culprit within an Eskimo community and force a confession. He could not strictly be called a sorcerer, because a sorcerer could be malevolent while a shaman seldom was evil. Another distinction was that shamans did not constitute a separate social class as the Christian clergy do. They lived, hunted, and dressed just like their fellow Eskimos. A shaman could be respected and even feared, but that depended on his personality. (If one was weak and inefficient, he

was ignored.) One became a shaman usually by receiving lessons from an elder shaman, but success also seemed to depend on time spent in solitude far from other men, fasting in the cold. Sometimes during those retreats a shaman would rub a small stone round and round a larger one until exhaustion and delirium deluded him into believing that he was really seeing spirits, and could therefore communicate with them.

# An Inuit Moral Tale

As an artist who produces social commentary paintings, I find it impossible to agree with some experts who condone Eskimo morality as a necessary natural phenomenon. Here are just a few samples of some former Eskimo customs I find repugnant: allowing the elderly to commit suicide, or in fact helping them to die; leaving baby girls outside the igloo to die; blood revenge for murder; exchanging wives. However the Eskimo does have a sense of justice, vindictive though it sometimes was, as expressed in the following tale:

In one settlement food was scarce. Two who suffered the most were a grandfather and his grandson, the only survivors of a family. They weren't strong enough to hunt, and no one would share food with them. Finally, the two decided they'd rather go out on a hunt and risk perishing than stay at home and slowly starve. They tracked down an enormous polar bear and followed him until, cornered against a glacier, he had to turn and fight. First the grandfather rushed at him with only a knife. The bear merely opened his cavernous mouth and the old man in his haste plunged in and was swallowed up.

The boy then charged with his harpoon. It would have gone badly for him too, were it not for the quick wits of the old man. He found the bear's stomach so hot that he determined to let in some fresh air. With one swift move he

slashed a hole in the stomach wall and out poured the steam. This of course killed the bear and the boy was saved. The two cut up the bear, and stashed the meat, which was enough to feed them all winter. The rest of the camp starved to death.

The moral of this story is obvious.

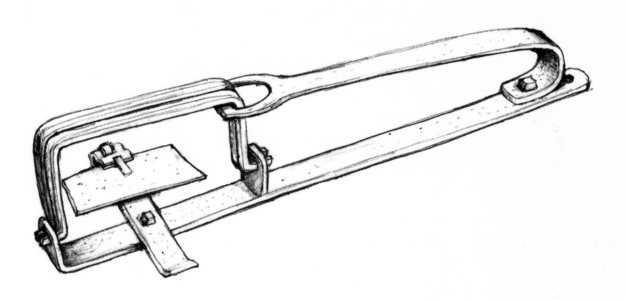

# Origin of the Constellation Pleiades

Toward the end of my first painting trip, to Cape Dorset, I turned to Terry Ryan's library for Eskimo subject matter. There I found Knud Rasmussen's book on the Inuit people, with several chapters devoted to Eskimo legends. They fascinated me. There were about as many stories explaining the origin of things as there were that gave a moral. This painting is an example of the first. Daylight in the Arctic during the winter months ranges from just a few hours to none at all. Therefore the Eskimos, like the Arabs, had a vast, dark, pollution-free sky to meditate on, and they devised names for all the major constellations. The one the Greeks named *Pleiades*, they have called the "Bear Hunters." This is how the myth goes:

> A polar bear came by an Eskimo camp in the dead of winter, and the men immediately gave chase with dogs and sleds. In the excitement of the pursuit, one of the boys on the head man's sled dropped his mitt. In order not to set back the chase, the head man shouted to him that since the moon was bright he should jump off to get the mitt and follow the sled track back home. However when the boy did get off, this lightened the load so that the sled began to rise. Then the other sleds began to rise too, and they all went up into the sky to become the group of stars known as the "Bear Hunters."

And there the story ends abruptly with no more mention of the boy or the bear.

# Children Admiring Crevasse in Alaska Glacier

Children are children everywhere, forever keen on exploration. Here I've depicted Alaskan Eskimo children admiring a crevasse in a glacier in much the same way as I used to lie down beside a spring of water bubbling up from the ground on the bog to the east of our Manitoba farm. I recall imagining vast subterranean caverns from which the water came. A glacier crevasse is very deep although its width may vary from only about a foot to more than sixty feet. Sometimes they are concealed from human eyes when windblown snow covers the top of the slit; an unsuspecting traveler may even fall in.

The danger does not make them less beautiful, however. Looking into such a fissure one can see that the rim with its closely packed snow is a dull eggshell white. Farther down where the snow has changed into ice the color is light green, then dark bottle-green. Finally, the eye can make out nothing more than the cold blue and inky black of the bottomless gulf.

# A Greenlandic Woman's Chores

In most Indian tribes the male has dominated the female, but in Eskimo society the situation is not so clear. True, a husband could be physically brutal to his wife. But according to Kaj Birket-Smith, an Arctic writer who lived with the Eskimos, there is a higher percentage of "henpecked" husbands among them than in many other societies.

To the white man, the lot of the Eskimo women appeared to be hard because she was seen doing the heavy work around the camp and home. When camp moving time came, the women would load the oomiak, a large skin-covered boat, with camp gear, children, dogs, in fact the works. The men would lead the way in their light kayaks while the women rowed the oomiaks. One Eskimo who was contemplating converting to Christianity was stunned when the priest said he'd have to limit himself to one wife: "But I need more than one woman to row my oomiak," he protested.

In a typical household day, the man of the house would set out on the hunt before dawn. He would breakfast on a piece of cold meat before he left, but his woman would have risen before him to light the lamp. After that, although it was still all mostly work, she could arrange her day to suit herself. One of her chores was to make the family's moccasins more supple by chewing them. The women of the camp would gossip together while they sewed or made baskets or cured skins. It was the woman's job to skin animals caught in the hunt, except for really large ones such as walrus. Some of the thinner, smaller skins also had to be chewed to remove stubborn fat.

70

Eskimo women were invariably skilled at sewing. The thread was made of split sinew but the kinds of stitches resembled those of hand-sewers in other parts of the world. The important thing to note is that, in the Arctic, sewing skill was critical: a well-made hunter's suit could make the difference between life or death out in a blizzard. It's not surprising therefore that husbands boasted of their wives' sewing skills over any other womanly attribute.

As the time approached for the hunter to return, his wife would put the cooking pot over the blubber lamp. The man expected food to be ready because apart from the cold breakfast, it would likely be his only meal of the day. As the man ate, his wife, using an ubiquitous woman's instrument called an "ulu," would skin the day's catch.

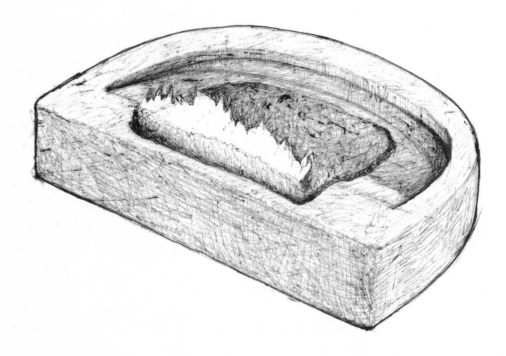

# An Eskimo Dice Game

Along with story-telling the Eskimo developed various indoor games to pass the long winter days. They were especially appreciated during storms when the menfolk were unable to venture out on the hunt.

Eskimos love games of chance. The dice game shown in this painting uses small seal bones, the trick being to see who could complete the interior of an igloo first. The dice doesn't have numbers on it but the go-ahead-and-build cue depends on which side of the bone lands uppermost. I have this group playing the game outdoors in the warmth of the sun shining on the south side of a snowdrift.

Another bone game which children played consisted of a rabbit skull tied to a pin with a thong. The idea was to toss the skull into the air and spear it with the pin. The number of points gained would depend upon which hole the player snagged.

Eskimo women also amused their children with "cat's-cradle" figures using a string and thong. Symbolically this was meant to entangle the sun and delay its departure. Such a game was confined therefore to autumn. Shadow games were supposed to be a kind of magic to catch the sun and hasten spring so they were usually played at the end of winter.

To foreigners looking from the outside in, the Eskimo people's lives looked to be rich in excitement, a notion probably conveyed by a very obvious struggle between life and death in the Arctic. But those outsiders who did sample the life style first-hand found it monotonous and restricted. Eskimos could

not read, for one thing. Apart from conversation and story-telling their pastimes had to be physical rather than intellectual. Dancing to the beat of drums was a physical community pastime but it depended on construction of a labyrinth of snow houses or on warm weather outside. Incidentally, the dances were more in the nature of a performance or competition. There was nothing comparable to our ballroom dancing or European folk dance in which the sexes mix.

# Ptarmigan, and Women Gathering Firewood

The Central Eskimos avoided the tree-line to the south, partly out of fear of the Indians, and concentrated their food-gathering efforts on the sea. This is why their camps frequently clung to the coast. But while they may have seemed indifferent to the stunted plants of the barren land, their lives still depended to some extent on the shrubs which dared grow there during the short Arctic summers. In winter, strange as it may seem, the shrubs' best protection was in fact the snow itself. Eskimo women would dig into those snowbanks for sled-loads of dwarf willow, their main fuel for cooking in the central Arctic.

In the picture I have a snow-white ptarmigan crouching beneath a dwarf willow, which lies gnarled and twisted close to the ground. The dwarf willow may be centuries old. So slowly, in fact, does it add its winter rings among the snowbanks, that these can only be seen under a microscope. Willow buds and twigs are the staple food of ptarmigans in winter. When one is killed, the Eskimo immediately slits the gizzard and intestines seeking the partly digested willow. This is considered a delicacy, and is extremely rich in Vitamin C which helps prevent the disease called scurvy.

Eskimos did the same thing with the partly-digested food found inside some of the sea animals that fed on seaweed. Thus indirectly the sea supplied the Eskimos with greens and nutrients that southerners usually get from lettuce, cabbage and fruit such as oranges.

# Story-Telling: A Winter Pastime

Story-telling helps relieve the tedium of seemingly endless winter nights. Eskimo stories could be of the latest catch or the prowess of hunters; they could teach a lesson to other members of the group or pass on a tradition. But legends were the most popular of all, and, surprisingly, these seemed to be fairly consistent across the North. There is a basic difference between Indian and Eskimo legends: Indians frequently used animals in their stories, but Eskimos invariably centered their legends around humans. Stories were told about the creation of lightning, of mist, of thunder, of rain, of the origin of whites and Indians, and a myriad of other topics.

The Eskimos knew their own land in great detail, but their concept of regions beyond the borders of the Arctic was very vague indeed. One of their legends concerns beings called "Skerries," who in their fickle nature sometimes helped people, but at other times carried them off to what we would call a prison. There are also legendary eye goblins, dwarfs, giants and shadow people. Below the visible world is an underworld where it is warm and comfortable. Some Eskimos go there, others into the skies where they play ball with a walrus head and cause the Northern Lights to appear. The Netsilik Eskimos also told of a third land of the dead, the "land of the crestfallen" just below the earth's crust. Unskilled hunters or women who have tattooed themselves clumsily would sit there, chin on chest, raising their heads now and then only to snap dully at passing butterflies, their only source of food.

# Harp Seal Pup Dozing After Feeding

A beautiful photograph of a harp seal pup, dozing in the sun after a feeding of milk from its mother, inspired this painting. The name of this species of seal derives from the coloring of the fur on the animal's back, the pattern resembling a harp. Seal pups are extraordinarily trusting and when sealers invade the ice floes in spring to seek out skins for persons of high fashion, the pups lie docilely on the ice until they are clubbed to death.

I was touched by a remark regarding seal pups made by a celebrated missionary to the Labrador Eskimos, Doctor Wilfred Grenfell. He compared the trusting quality of seal pups to the willing sacrifice of Christ, the Lamb of God who gave up his life as a ransom for mankind.

Seal hunting in this manner has created great controversy among conservationists, animal lovers, and those whose livelihood depends on it. Still, each year the hunt goes on. Apart from his religious respect for animals, the Eskimo cannot afford to be sentimental. One has only to consider the absurdity of expecting an Eskimo to be a vegetarian. A great difference between white man and the Eskimo (before white man's arrival in the North) was that the white hunter was sometimes motivated by greed, but the Eskimo's only motivation was hunger.

# Copper Eskimo Cod Fishing

The Eskimo has a variety of methods of catching fish and they vary from one part of the Arctic to the other. The method I've shown here is used by the Coppermine River Eskimos of the central Arctic.

When the lakes are frozen, the fish are caught with a jig lowered through a hole chopped in the ice. The fish are enticed to the surface by means of shining pieces of metal jiggled up and down, or by models of fish carved from ivory or pieces of fish skin. The hook is unbarbed, for the Eskimo nabs the fish behind the gills and pulls it out onto the ice.

Perhaps the reader may wonder why the fisherman then lines up his catch in the peculiar circular position I've shown in the painting. The Eskimo believes all animals have souls; he feels he must be polite to whatever he kills for then it will help him catch others. After the cod has its flesh eaten, its soul will return to the lake, and enter the body of another fish, prepared to be caught again. The fisherman also believes that if he lays the fish in a circle around him, heads toward the hole, then he will always be in the midst of a school of fish.

In summer, hand-made spears are also used to catch fish. The spear is fashioned in the shape of a trident, except that the middle tooth is shorter than the others, and not barbed but needle-like. The side prongs are barbed and flexible, better to hold the fish until it is clubbed and removed from the spear. In that type of fishing, a line of fishermen may straddle a stream each with his own spear to catch as many as he can when a run of fish comes along.

# Hunter Stranded on an Ice Floe

One of the most terrifying experiences a hunter can have is being stranded on an ice floe. It might occur when he is alone and takes risks pursuing a seal, jumping from floe to floe. Sometimes he is so anxious for food he has not enough time to properly assess his chances of returning to land. It is a truly desperate situation: to let himself fall into the water or to attempt to swim is unthinkable, for the intensely cold water means certain death. No matter how well his clothes are made they afford no protection whatsoever. Also there's the agonizing question of which way the drift will go—toward land? Out to sea? When will the floe break up, reducing the standing space until his weight tips the ice? Dare he hope that the weather turns much colder so that the sea freezes and he can simply walk off?

An Eskimo is marvellously patient and brave, a product of many hunting experiences, but there is nothing to be done in this circumstance, except wait. While waiting in his solitude would he lapse into despair, or pray to the Great Spirit? Would he sit quietly to conserve his strength or stand up and shout to the empty skies? I asked the Reverend Mike Gardener, the Anglican minister at Pangnirtung, what an Eskimo would do in such a situation. He said: "Pray." "But what about before the coming of Christianity?" I asked. Mike admitted he didn't know what would have taken place.

# Legend about the Origin of White Men

From time immemorial the Eskimos and Indians have been hostile to each other. This hostility between them did not take the form of full open warfare, but of stealthy ambush and isolated raids. The Eskimos are, by necessity and inclination, peaceful. Just as the Russians in part defeated Germany and France by retreating and relying on winter to assist them, so the Eskimo coped with Indian inroads. By choice of environment the Indians were forest-dwellers. The Eskimos feared the forest and felt safe and were content in the treeless tundra. Both peoples now feel a common bond under the pressure of the white man's culture and technology, but the Eskimos' ancient atavistic terror of the Indians persists, coming out in their dreams as bogeymen do in a child's subconscious mind.

The word Eskimo is really an Indian word meaning "eaters of raw meat." The Eskimos themselves, however, prefer to be called by their own name Inuit which means "the people." In other words there are human beings (themselves), and others, namely the Indians and white men. In their legends the latter two are considered as bastard descendants of an Eskimo woman who mated with a dog. The story goes that a beautiful Inuit maid kept rejecting the courtship of even the handsomest and best young hunters in the village. Finally the father threatened that she'd have to be satisfied with his dog for a mate. One night a handsome stranger came to the igloo and was accepted by both the girl and her parents, but in the morning the stranger was gone and only when the maid showed signs of pregnancy did it dawn on the father that it had been his dog who had assumed

human shape (as animals sometimes do in Eskimo legends). As the time of her delivery approached the father could bear his revulsion no longer and banished her to a small desolate island where, true to his fears, she gave birth not to a single child but to a whole litter. The island was so small and desolate she could not support her half-human, half-animal children and set them adrift in boats hoping they would reach their salvation. One boat-load went south and it is from these that the Indians are descended. The other went east and gave rise to the whites. To the Eskimos the white man has always appeared restless, time obsessed, ambitious, boorish. These traits they excused with the explanation that the boat their mother put them in leaked and they had to frantically bail it out — that is why they are always in a hurry and have much to do.

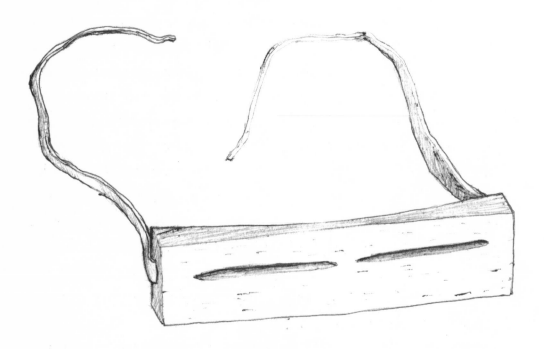

# Starvation in the Arctic

"To every thing there is a season, and a time to every purpose under heaven: A time to be born and a time to die."

Ecclesiastes 3:1-2

The Eskimo has always lived in harmony with his world. And the reality of that world has always been that Nature sometimes conspires against man and animal and sometimes blesses them. The white man is always anticipating such things as shortages of food, and has long been aware of the laws of balance in Nature. But the Eskimo either didn't know, or care, about these balances and thus had to accept famine as well as feast in due course. The white man too had trouble aplenty before he plotted the course of Nature, but his survival skills proved greater than those of the Eskimo, despite the latter's sometimes amazing hunting ingenuity. In the end, the Eskimo was forced to admit dependence on the white man.

In the primitive, pre-white times, the Eskimo strained his every wit and muscle to the utmost to provide for his family. He could store no corn or berries as even his feared southern neighbor, the Indian, did, because nothing grew in his barren land. Meat certainly could be kept during the long winter, but he knew no methods of refrigeration to get a supply of meat through the short, hot summer.

Inevitably, there were times when their courage and hunting skills simply proved in vain. Whole communities would die. I have here depicted such a family after it's all over and the igloo begins to fall in.

The beginning of the end had come when the family began to slowly consume whatever small reserves of food they had on hand. The next step was trying to gain meager sustenance by eating much of their leather clothing. At that time the family members began to die one by one. The desperate survivors resorted to cannibalism, carving flesh off the bodies of those already dead. Finally all movement ceased . . . the cruel land had won.

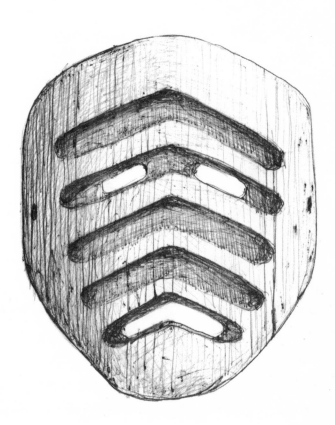

# Glacier, and Snowy Owl Hunting Lemming

Most people know from natural history studies that animal populations follow cycles and thus a balance is kept. Nowhere is this more starkly evident than in the North.

A good part of this cyclical ebb and flow is connected to an animal called the lemming. Eskimos call him *Kilangmiutak*, "one who comes from the sky." When these animals appear in such huge numbers it seems they must surely fall from heaven. In absolutely ideal conditions the female lemming can produce as many as sixteen litters in a year, the offspring in turn growing to mating size in less than a month. True, winter slows them down in the Arctic, but they can still produce five to six litters in the brief, northern summer. At their low cycle, there may be only one lemming for every ten acres; at their peak the population explodes to as many as fifty per acre, an acre that is honeycombed with as many as four thousand burrows. Everywhere one can hear the squeak and chatter of these excited, irritable animals that spill across the terrain in successive migrations, and end up literally committing suicide by drowning when they are confronted by a large body of water. They strip the vegetation, but by loosening the tundra and fertilizing it with their droppings they improve plant growth for the next season. That in turn nourishes larger animals such as musk-oxen and caribou, on which man feeds.

The cycle of the snowy owl fits into, or rather depends on, the lemming cycle. After a peak lemming year has passed the owls lay fewer eggs, and of those that hatch, they feed only one or two. The snowy owl's search for food at such a time has been known to take it as far south as Toronto.

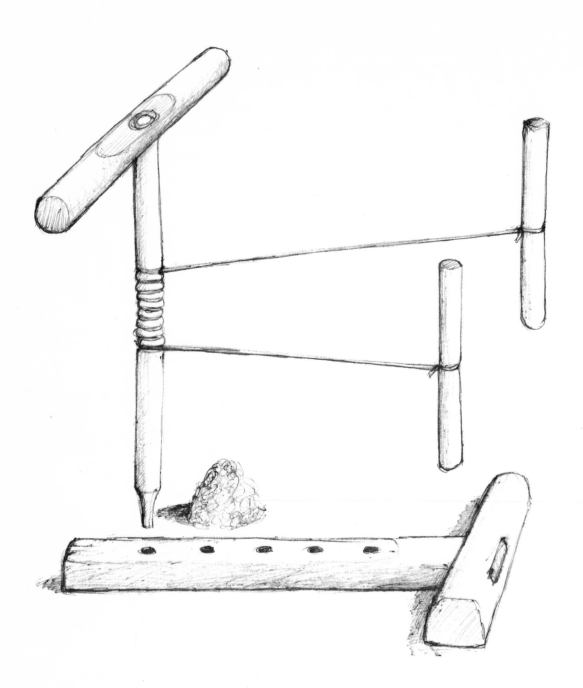